WILLIAM SHAKESPEARE

adapted by Jon Blake

OXFORD
UNIVERSITY PRESS
Great Clarendon Street, Oxford OX2 6DP

Oxford University Press is a department of the University of Oxford.
It furthers the University's objective of excellence in research, scholarship,
and education by publishing worldwide in

Oxford New York
Auckland Cape Town Dar es Salaam Hong Kong Karachi
Kuala Lumpur Madrid Melbourne Mexico City Nairobi
New Delhi Sanghai Taipei Toronto

With offices in

Argentina Austria Brazil Chile Czech Republic France Greece
Guatemala Hungary Italy Japan Poland Portugal Singapore
South Korea Switzerland Thailand Turkey Ukraine Vietnam

First published 2001
This edition published 2006

British Library Cataloguing in Publication Data
Data available

ISBN: 978-0-19-918492-7

15 17 19 20 18 16 14

Cover: Mark Edwards
Inside illustrations: Martin Cottam

Printed in Malaysia by MunSang Printers Sdn Bhd

Paper used in the production of this book is a natural, recyclable product
made from wood grown in sustainable forests. The manufacturing process
conforms to the environmental regulations of the country of origin.

About the Author

WILLIAM SHAKESPEARE
1564 – 1616

William Shakespeare was born in Stratford-upon-Avon, the son of a glovemaker. By the age of 28 he was living in London as an actor and playwright. In 1598 he began writing for the new Globe Theatre. Thirty-five plays, and great success, followed. Theatre in those days was as popular as films are today.

Macbeth was written in 1606. As with most of his plays, Shakespeare got the story from somewhere else – a historian called Holinshed. The real Macbeth came to the throne of Scotland in 1040, ruled successfully, and was killed in 1057. But Shakespeare wasn't too interested in historical facts – he wanted to create a good story. He turned Macbeth into a tragic villain, poisoned by ambition. The play is full of dramatic action, strong characters, and memorable speeches. *Macbeth* remains one of Shakespeare's most popular plays.

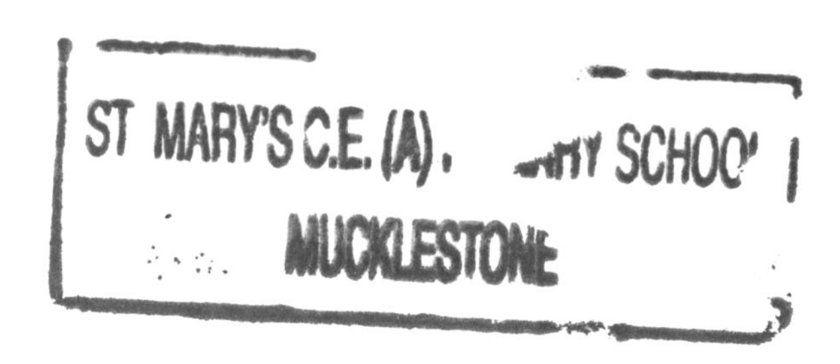

CONTENTS

CHAPTER I

A Bloody Battle and a Dangerous Prophecy

This is a story of ambition, blood, and vile, vile weather. Its setting is the bare and bitter **heaths** of Scotland, and its villains . . . well, you'll hear about them soon enough.

As for me – never mind my name. I am, I think, fifteen years old. I was born with marks upon me which some called signs of witchcraft. When sickness came to the village I was blamed, tormented, and sentenced to death. I escaped and fled to the wild heath, to live on berries and to spend my life watching.

Most of all I watch those women they call the Weird Sisters because, like me, they are called witches. The sisters have the knowledge I seek. They can conjure up storms, cast curses on their enemies, and greatest of all, foretell the future.

It was from the sisters that I first heard the name Macbeth. What a foul day that was! Thunder rattled the heavens and fog smothered the heath like a **shroud**. The sisters danced wildly, screaming about a bloody battle and showing off a hacked-off thumb. Again and again they shrieked the name 'Macbeth'.

As the sisters melted into the fog I crept forward to view their glass. Within this sacred object all things on earth could be seen – or, at least, all things the sisters wished to see.

With heart beating hard I steadied my eye. First I saw the fluttering flags of the King of Norway, then the face of Cawdor, the traitor lord, in arms against the Scots king, Duncan. Suddenly, confusion filled the glass, then horror. Screams, curses, and blasting cannons out-roared the thunder. I saw horsemen with axes hacking. I saw limbs chopped from bodies. I watched living people dropping like dumb puppets. Then, in the midst of it all, I spied a superman.

He stood like a rock in a heaving sea, slashing and hacking with awesome power. Alone, it seemed, he turned the tide. The flags of Norway turned and fled, and the day was Scotland's.

Soon I was to crouch within a few yards of the hero of this battle.

One dark evening, the Weird Sisters gathered at their appointed place. By and by a tired army arrived, creaking and clanking across the rainswept heath. Out of their number rode two men, one our hero. Seeing the sisters, they came to a halt. They had seen many horrors that day, but nothing quite like these wild and bearded women.

'All **hail**, Macbeth!' cried the first sister. 'Hail to thee, **Thane** of Glamis!'

So this was Macbeth! I felt **awe** and a sense of foreboding.

'All hail, Macbeth!' cried the second sister. 'Hail to thee, Thane of Cawdor.'

Macbeth's brow furrowed. What were the sisters saying? He was not the Thane of Cawdor!

'All hail, Macbeth,' cried the third sister, 'that shall be king hereafter!'

King? Macbeth? What kind of prophecy was this? thought Macbeth.

'And what of me?' asked Macbeth's companion.

'Hail, Banquo!' cried the first sister. 'Lesser than Macbeth, and greater.'

'Not so happy,' chimed the second, 'yet much happier.'

'Thou shalt make kings,' intoned the third, 'though thou shalt not rule.'

With that, the Weird Sisters melted into the fog, leaving the two men baffled.

Were the women real, or just a dream? What was the meaning of their **prophecies**? The Thane of Cawdor was alive, and so was Duncan, the king!

'We must have been drugged,' said Banquo.

'Or mad, to believe that nonsense,' replied Macbeth. But the truth was, he liked what the sisters had told him. The idea of being king tempted him greatly.

CHAPTER 2

The First Prophecy Fulfilled

Unlike Macbeth, I had learned to respect the sisters' prophecies. Full of expectation, I watched for the story to unfold. It was not long before the king's messenger reached Macbeth. From the messenger Macbeth learnt how his own reputation had soared.

'King Duncan is keen to repay your efforts,' said the messenger.

'How?' asked Macbeth, eagerly.

'With a new title,' replied the messenger.

'And what might that be?' asked Macbeth.

'Thane of Cawdor,' replied the messenger.

These words were like a blinding sun to Macbeth. 'But the Thane of Cawdor still lives,' he objected.

'His title has been stripped from him,' replied the messenger. 'He awaits trial for high treason.'

Macbeth thanked the messenger, and to his face remained calm. But the moment the messenger was gone, Macbeth seized Banquo by the wrist.

'Those hags spoke the truth!' he hissed.

'Maybe,' replied Banquo, still unconvinced.

'Don't you want your children to be kings?' urged Macbeth. 'That was part of the same prophecy!'

'Maybe they already knew about Cawdor,' replied Banquo. 'Maybe they gave us that little truth to poison our minds – to win us to some devious plan of theirs.'

Macbeth heard the words, but was not listening to the meaning. Inside his head thoughts raged like a storm. The hope of being king had taken root in him. But how? Would he have to make it happen himself? Or should he simply wait for fortune to play its hand?

'Macbeth?' asked Banquo. 'Are you with us?'

Macbeth broke out of his private thoughts, and the two set off with their comrades in the direction of King Duncan.

'Listen, Banquo,' whispered Macbeth. 'Let's think over what's happened today, then speak our minds freely to each other.'

'Gladly,' replied Banquo.

I rested my eyes from the glass and laughed gently to myself. Macbeth's darkest thoughts might be known to me, but to Banquo? That would never be.

CHAPTER 3

Thoughts of Murder

Cawdor did his best to save his skin. He admitted every wrongdoing, repented like a saint, and begged his king for pardon. It did him no good. He was executed, like all traitors.

Macbeth, on the other hand, was showered with praise. Duncan could not do enough for his cousin, the saviour of his kingdom.

'I've not valued you enough, Macbeth,' he said.

'It is reward enough to do my duty,' replied Macbeth, sounding like the humblest subject in the kingdom.

'To think I'd trusted Cawdor,' continued the king.

'Two-faced dog,' replied Macbeth.

'Indeed,' agreed Duncan. 'To look at him, you could never have guessed his devious thoughts.'

'Indeed,' agreed Macbeth.

An important announcement was in the air that day. You needed no magic glass to guess what it was about. Duncan was ageing, and had not yet announced his successor. Now, at last, the question would be settled.

Macbeth stood at Duncan's right hand as the king began to speak. The hot grip of ambition was tightening on his throat.

'Sons, **kinsmen**, thanes,' began the king. 'Today is a day of reward for many of you: new lands, new titles. But as for my state and throne, that can only fall upon one man . . . my son, Malcolm, who I hereby name, Prince of Cumberland.'

A cackle escaped my throat as the self-satisfied smile vanished from Macbeth's face. Now he had two hurdles to overcome on his way to the throne. No wonder he departed the court in such agitation!

◆◆◆

I was not the only female watching these events unfold. Away in Inverness, pacing the corridors of a cold castle, was Macbeth's keen-eyed wife. Lady Macbeth had heard all the news from Macbeth's letters. With each one she grew hungrier for power. There were no battles or cheering crowds to enliven her empty life. The prospect of becoming queen, on the other hand – that was a road to glory.

Just as I knew Macbeth's mind, so I knew his wife's. I had been tormented and driven from society by hard-faced women like her. But she was still not hard enough for the job in hand. For that she needed special help. I watched intently as she summoned the spirits and called on them to destroy her human tenderness: to turn her into a machine for murder.

As Lady Macbeth's heart hardened, her thoughts turned to her husband. For all his fierceness in battle, Macbeth was still too soft for this business. She would have to destroy his conscience too. Then the crown would be theirs for the taking.

The opportunity came sooner than Lady Macbeth could have dreamt. News reached the castle that Macbeth was on his way – and close behind him, the grateful Duncan. The king was to be their guest that night.

Lady Macbeth embraced her husband. There was no need for Macbeth to ask if the letters had reached her.

'The king,' asked Lady Macbeth, 'how long is he staying?'

''Til tomorrow morning,' replied Macbeth.

Lady Macbeth's face set like stone. 'Then we must ensure he never sees that morning,' she pronounced.

'What do you mean?' asked Macbeth, nervously.

'You know exactly what I mean,' replied Lady Macbeth.

Lady Macbeth had her way. The trap was readied, and sweetened with delicious meats and wines. Duncan rode into it as innocent as a dove – but then, why should he suspect the cousin who had just saved his throne? Or his charming wife, who had gone to such trouble to cater for her king and his attendants? Such a fair and noble woman she was.

Yes, Duncan feasted well that night, but Macbeth was in no mood to eat. He paced his rooms, then his grounds, building himself up for the dark deed. The more he thought about it, the greater the doubts became. What kind of host would murder a man who had come to him for protection? Besides, murdering Duncan did not guarantee the crown for Macbeth. The king was a popular leader, a modest, decent man – his killer would not be honoured, but cursed.

Lady Macbeth, on the other hand, was having no such pangs of conscience. With urgent steps she sought out her husband.

'There you are!' she cried. 'What do you think you are doing, leaving the banqueting hall?'

'Has Duncan noticed?' asked Macbeth.

'Of course he has noticed!' replied his wife.

Macbeth steeled himself. 'We're not going through with this,' he said.

'Don't say that,' murmured Lady Macbeth.

'All my life I have craved the respect I have today,' replied Macbeth. 'To throw it away now . . . '

Lady Macbeth's face seemed agonized. 'Were you drunk when you said you would be king?' she hissed. 'Maybe when you said you loved me you were drunk as well! What is wrong with you? The greatest glory in life is there for the taking, but you're too scared to grasp it. You'd rather be a second-rater – a meek little nobody!'

‘I’m being a man,’ replied Macbeth.

‘A man?’ cried his wife. ‘A man has the courage of his convictions! And think how more of a man you’ll be when you’ve gone through with this. Believe me, I am a woman, I know what love a woman feels when she nurses a baby, but I’d dash its brains out for a chance like this.’

‘And what if we fail?’ countered Macbeth.

‘We will not fail,’ replied Lady Macbeth, with steely certainty.

Macbeth was impressed by his wife’s determination. Sensing she was winning him, Lady Macbeth pressed on with her plans.

‘Duncan is sure to sleep heavily tonight,’ she said, ‘and I shall deal with his guards. A little charm . . . a few songs . . . a bottle or two . . . I’ll see to it they drink themselves into a stupor. There’ll be nothing to stop us getting to Duncan – and laying the blame on them to boot.’

Macbeth turned the plan over in his mind. ‘We could use their daggers,’ he suggested, ‘and mark them with his blood.’

Lady Macbeth smiled, and laid her hand on her husband’s. ‘Exactly,’ she replied. ‘And the way we will grieve for Duncan, no one will dare to suspect our involvement.’

Macbeth was won over. The desire to murder, like an iron mask, came down over his human features. From this point, there was no going back.

CHAPTER 4

The Dark Deed is Done

It was a bleak night, that fatal night. No moon, no stars, a cruel wind and rain that drove into every cranny of Glamis Castle. Banquo was awake with the night owls – afraid to fall asleep and dream dangerous fantasies. His nerve was shaken; at the sound of footsteps he seized his sword.

'Who's there?' he cried.

'A friend,' replied Macbeth.

Banquo relaxed a little at the sight of his old companion. 'Not yet asleep?' he noted.

'I was making sure everything was all right with Duncan,' replied Macbeth.

'Oh, he seems happy enough,' said Banquo.

There was an unsettled silence.

'I dreamt about the Weird Sisters last night,' said Banquo.

'I've put them out of my mind,' replied Macbeth.

'I wish I could,' said Banquo.

Another difficult silence.

'Banquo,' began Macbeth, softly, 'if you do throw

your lot in with me . . . you will do well out of it.'

'Certainly,' replied Banquo. 'As long as I do nothing dishonest.'

It was not the reply Macbeth wanted. Banquo was just too honourable. He would never make a reliable ally.

'Well . . . ' concluded Macbeth. 'Sleep well.'

'And you,' replied Banquo.

With that, Banquo departed. The coast was clear.

Macbeth awaited a signal from his wife, who at that very moment was handing the drunken guards a little nightcap: hot spiced milk – mixed with a little something to help them get a good night's rest. The mixture did its work quickly; both men slumped into a sleep so deep, they seemed more like the lifeless bodies on the battlefield. Calm and focused, Lady Macbeth removed their daggers and laid them ready for Macbeth, then gave two rings on a bell. Her part was done.

Macbeth was not so calm. As he had stood waiting, the vision of a dagger had appeared, hovering before his eyes. Macbeth made to grasp it – but his hand closed on thin air. Back came the vision, this time clotted with blood. It was as if someone somewhere knew what was about to happen.

The sound of the bell broke the dagger's spell. Macbeth was like a trained beast. He moved ghost-like through the castle, 'til he reached the sleeping guards. He secured both their blades beneath his belt. Then he lifted the latch on Duncan's **bedchamber** and slipped inside.

The old king certainly was sleeping well. He lay on his back in the great oak bed; hair and beard spread out over the bedclothes, snoring gently. Macbeth approached in the dim light, heart pounding. In sleep, Duncan looked almost angelic.

Macbeth slipped a guard's knife from his belt. It was best not to think too long. In one swift movement, Macbeth swept back his arm and landed the dagger full force. From the king there came a last pitiful sigh as the life rushed out of his punctured soul. Then, out of nowhere, came the sound of laughter. Macbeth froze over the grisly picture he had created. He heard a word: 'Murder!' . . . hushed and urgent conversation . . . muttered prayers. 'God bless us!' came a voice. 'Amen!' came another. By instinct, Macbeth sought to add his own 'Amen!' but nothing would come. The word would not leave his throat.

In haste, Macbeth backed out of the chamber of death and hurried to his own rooms, still bearing the daggers.

Lady Macbeth met him with thirsty, anxious eyes.

'Is it done?' she demanded.

Macbeth's mind was in chaos. 'Yes, yes,' he gabbled. 'Did you hear a noise?'

'An owl,' replied his wife.

'No, human voices!' snapped Macbeth. 'Who lies in the second chamber?'

'Donalbain, Duncan's younger son,' replied Lady Macbeth.

Macbeth stared at his bloody hands. 'This is a sorry sight,' he muttered.

'Not for us,' replied his wife.

'I heard someone laugh,' hissed Macbeth. 'And someone cried, "Murder!" Then I heard prayers, and "God bless us!" but I could not say "Amen!" I, who have most need of blessing, could not say, "Amen!"'

'Enough of this,' said Lady Macbeth.

'Then I swear I heard, "Sleep no more – Macbeth hath murdered sleep – Macbeth will sleep no more!"'

'Enough!' cried Lady Macbeth. 'Now wash your hands. Why have you brought the daggers here? Put them back with the guards, and smear them both with blood.'

'I can't go back there,' gasped Macbeth.

'For pity's sake!' cried Lady Macbeth. 'Give them to me – I'll do it!'

So Lady Macbeth took charge, leaving her husband staring hopelessly at his hands, wondering if the stain could ever be washed from them.

CHAPTER 5

Witnesses of Death

Never had the kingdom known such a night of storms. Chimneys were sent smashing; trees were snapped and seized by bloated rivers; the sea cast boulders at the trembling shore. Across the heaths the wind wailed a sad and eerie song, the sky cried endlessly, and the very land shuddered. It was weather to gladden a Weird Sister's heart.

Out of this foul night came Macduff and Lennox, two noblemen. They were battered by the storm and unsettled by eerie sounds from the darkness – the screeching of owls, the muttering of prophecies, and strange screams of death. With relief they arrived at Macbeth's gate and hammered for entry.

Old Pickspot the gate porter woke with a jump. 'All right, all right,' he muttered. 'Knock, knock, knock, what a racket!' He took down his keys, called for Maggot, the wolfhound, and made his way across the courtyard like an ambling old tortoise.

'Knock, knock. Who's there? Boo. Boo who? No need to cry, mate, I only want to come in!'

Macduff and Lennox, soaked to the bones, hammered

ever harder.

'All right, I said,' mumbled Pickspot. 'Blimey, aren't some people impatient?' With fumbling hands he sorted out the right key, and five minutes later the gate was open. Macduff and Lennox were not amused.

'What time were you up to, that you sleep so late?' grumbled Macduff.

'I really couldn't say,' replied Pickspot. 'The sundial never seems to work at night.'

Lennox frowned. 'What kind of fool are you?' he snarled.

'That's a very good question,' replied Pickspot. 'Let me answer it with a story. Yesterday I asked the sergeant for a shovel. He brought me two, and told me to take my pick. "I don't see a pick, sir," I replied. "Only two shovels!"'

'For pity's sake!' cried Macduff. 'Let us in!'

Old Pickspot moved aside, and the two men advanced, only to come face to face with Maggot.

'Does your dog bite?' asked Lennox.

'Indeed not,' replied Pickspot.

Lennox moved forward. Maggot bared its fangs, leapt up, and bit his arm.

'I thought you said your dog didn't bite!' cried Lennox.

'That's the sergeant's dog,' replied Pickspot.

The old porter was living dangerously. Fortunately for him, at that moment, his master strode into the courtyard.

'Macbeth!' cried Macduff. 'Thank heaven for that!'

'Good morrow, both,' proclaimed Macbeth.

'Good morrow, worthy Thane,' replied Macduff. 'Is the king stirring?'

'Not yet,' said Macbeth.

'He asked me to call early on him,' explained Macduff.

Macbeth remained calm. Clearly he had pulled himself together. 'He sleeps through there,' he said, indicating to the door behind which the night's evil had been done.

Macduff set off to wake the king. His innocence did not last long. Moments later he was back, his skin grey, his eyes frantic.

'Oh, horror!' he cried. 'Nameless horror!'

'What's the matter?' cried Macbeth.

'Murder!' cried Macduff.

'Not the king?' blurted Lennox.

'Go . . . ' gasped Macduff. 'See . . . '

Macbeth and Lennox raced across the courtyard, leaving Macduff staggering like a drunk, yelling for others to awake. Enter Banquo, closely followed by Lady Macbeth, her face a picture of innocence.

'Duncan is murdered!' cried Macduff.

'In our house?' cried Lady Macbeth. 'Say it's not so!'

Malcolm and Donalbain, the king's sons, were next on the scene. For all Macbeth's fears, they seemed to have heard nothing of the murder. Macduff broke the news to

them just as Macbeth and Lennox returned from the king's chamber.

'Who did this thing?' asked Malcolm, stiff with shock.

'We found the king's guards spattered with blood,' replied Lennox. 'Their daggers were beside them, still unwiped.'

'And you left them there?' said Macduff.

'I killed them,' replied Macbeth.

'Killed them?' repeated Macduff. 'Why did you not interrogate them?'

'Was I supposed to remain calm?' asked Macbeth. 'I had just seen the body of our king, slaughtered like an animal! And there were his murderers, without a shred of guilt, sleeping with his blood on their knives! What kind of man could have contained his fury?'

The king's sons did not look convinced. It was time for Lady Macbeth to show off her acting ability. She staggered against the wall in a dramatic swoon. 'Help me!' she whimpered. Immediately all the courteous gentlemen forgot Macbeth, rushed to her aid, and carried her off to her chamber.

Banquo, however, was not so easily thrown off the scent. 'We must uncover the source of this treason,' he pronounced.

'Indeed,' agreed Macbeth. He glanced into his old comrade's eyes, and saw that they were full of suspicion.

CHAPTER 6

No Rest for the Wicked

Malcolm had been named Duncan's heir, and by rights should have taken the throne. But Malcolm was young, and full of fear. Whoever had killed Duncan was surely after his blood also, and that of Donalbain. The two resolved to slip unnoticed from the castle and flee: Malcolm to England, Donalbain to Ireland. There they would find new allies, for in Scotland they could trust nobody – least of all their closest relative, Macbeth.

The sons' escape was a double blessing to Macbeth. The last obstacles to the throne were removed – and Macbeth had two prime suspects to blame for Duncan's murder. They had everything to gain from it. And why else would they flee with such haste?

So it was that Macbeth was crowned at Scone. Duncan's body was carried to the Isle of Iona, to be buried alongside the kings of old, while his humble subjects wept rivers of tears.

It was dark as night on the day of Macbeth's **coronation**. You might have expected a bolt of lightning as Lady Macbeth accepted the queen's crown, but no. There were rumours, however, that Duncan's horses had gone wild, broken out of their stalls, and turned cannibal. It was not the only story of unnatural acts. One farmer told the tale of a falcon killed by an owl. All over nature, it seemed, lesser creatures were murdering their betters.

So, the murderous couple had achieved their goal. Wealth, power, and prestige were theirs. Such a shame that Macbeth could not enjoy his success. His mind was riddled with guilt. Nor could he rest an instant, knowing Duncan's sons were telling all England and Ireland that he was a murderer. Then there was the prophecy of the Weird Sisters to Banquo: 'Thou shalt make kings, though thou shalt not rule.' In other words, Banquo's sons would be the future rulers of Scotland.

Macbeth had come to fear and loathe his old comrade. Though Macbeth was king, Banquo seemed so much more noble in his nature. Banquo was not only brave, but honest and intelligent. He commanded the respect of others in a way that Macbeth never would. The thought of Banquo's sons succeeding to the throne was unbearable. Macbeth had not gone to the trouble of murdering Duncan for their benefit.

Clearly, something had to be done about Banquo.

CHAPTER 7

Macbeth Wades Deeper into Blood

Lady Macbeth had always wanted to host the most lavish banquets in the land. Now, at last it was possible. The feast she had thrown for Duncan was nothing compared to the one planned to celebrate Macbeth's coronation.

Every lord and lady in Scotland was invited to the banquet. Tables were laid with silver, new tapestries hung, hogs and deer slaughtered, butts of wine brought in by the dozen. If the queen was short of anything, she simply demanded it of her people. Such was the power of the crown.

Every feast must have a chief guest – and who better than Macbeth's bravest ally, Banquo?

'Your attendance is expected,' said Macbeth, to his old friend, in the presence of the other guests.

'I am at your majesty's command,' replied Banquo. As always, he acted dutifully, but it was as if the two were playing a game. Banquo suspected Macbeth had blood on his hands, and Macbeth knew that Banquo suspected. But neither could speak honestly.

'We are so pleased,' said Lady Macbeth, with her false and charming smile. 'The table would seem empty

without you.'

'I'm flattered,' replied Banquo.

Macbeth's eyes narrowed. 'So,' he said, 'will you be riding this afternoon?'

'Aye, my good lord,' replied Banquo.

'I was hoping to ask your opinion on a few matters today,' said Macbeth, 'but never mind – it can wait 'til tomorrow. Tell me – are you riding far?'

'As far as necessary,' replied Banquo, 'to fill up the time between now and supper.'

'After dark, then?' asked Macbeth.

'Indeed,' replied Banquo.

'And your son, Fleance,' continued Macbeth. 'Will he be going?'

'He will,' replied Banquo.

'Excellent,' said Macbeth. 'Well, enjoy your ride, and whatever you do, don't miss the feast!'

'Never fear, my good lord,' replied Banquo. 'I shall be there.'

Macbeth watched Banquo exit, then turned to the others present. 'You must all amuse yourselves 'til supper,' he said. 'I want some time alone – then I shall enjoy your company all the more this evening.'

Lady Macbeth and the guests departed, leaving Macbeth alone with his attendant.

'The men I asked for,' said Macbeth. 'Are they at the gate?'

'They are, my lord,' replied the attendant.

'Bring them in,' demanded Macbeth.

Two grim-faced soldiers were brought before Macbeth. The attendant departed; Macbeth lowered his voice.

'Have you considered the things we spoke of earlier?' asked Macbeth.

The two men nodded. I read their faces, and saw a deep grudge lurking there.

'You were promised promotion,' continued Macbeth, 'but the promises came to nothing. You thought it was I who frustrated you, but you were wrong. The man who stood between you and your ambitions was Banquo.'

'So you have said,' replied Bell, the first man.

'I have,' continued Macbeth, 'but I went further than that. I asked you to do something for me. That is the reason we meet today, is it not?'

The two men said nothing.

'Of course,' said Macbeth, with a sneer, 'you can always be good Christians and forgive Banquo for stabbing you in the back.'

'We are men!' replied Black, the second man.

'So you are,' said Macbeth, 'as greyhounds and spaniels and flea-bitten mongrels are all dogs. The point is, what kind of men are you?'

'Men who have been pushed too far,' replied Bell.

'Men prepared to do anything,' replied Black.

'Well,' said Macbeth, 'we three have a common enemy. I could, of course, have Banquo swept from my sight . . . but I have friends who are also Banquo's friends. I don't want to fall out with them. For this reason it is better that I am not seen to be involved in Banquo's misfortune – you understand?'

'Your wish is our command,' replied Black.

Macbeth clamped his arms around the shoulders of the two veterans. 'You are good men,' he pronounced. 'Within the hour I'll advise you where to hide yourselves. You must be some distance from the palace, and under cover of darkness. I expect a professional job – no botch-ups. And remember – Fleance must be dealt with at the same time.'

'We understand,' said Bell.

'We're ready,' added Black.

'Excellent,' replied Macbeth. 'Await my call.'

For once the sky was clear, as Banquo set out with Fleance that day. They would take the trail beside the **loch**, then between the craggy hills and through the forest. Fleance led the way; Banquo glowed with pride at the expert horsemanship of his growing son. He had not forgotten the Weird Sisters' prophecy that his sons would be kings. Like any good father, his hopes were high for his child.

Back at the palace, meanwhile, Lady Macbeth was tormented with discontent. A great night lay ahead of her, but uncertainties lay all around her. Not that she would show any weakness to her husband . . . when she could find him.

'You're spending too much time alone,' she said. 'Thinking too much.'

Macbeth said nothing.

'It's no good dwelling on the past,' continued his wife. 'What's done is done.'

'But it isn't done,' replied Macbeth. 'That's the problem. If it was done, maybe I could sleep without these damned nightmares. Better to be dead than to be tortured like this.'

'Please, my lord,' said Lady Macbeth. 'Put a smile on your face. We don't want the guests seeing you like this.'

'Don't worry,' replied Macbeth. 'I shall put on a good act for them. And you, for your part, must be sure to give Banquo your best attention.'

These words came as a surprise to me; for a moment I thought I had misunderstood Macbeth's conversation with the two veterans. But I soon realized that Lady Macbeth knew nothing of the plot to kill Banquo. It was better for her to remain ignorant – she would be grateful enough when the news broke.

CHAPTER 8

An Unexpected Guest

Dusk thickened. The starlings gathered and the crows took flight into the woods. Macbeth's hired men waited.

At length there came the sound of two horses. All the other expected guests were safely at the palace – the riders could only be Banquo and Fleance. Sure enough, it was Banquo's voice that called out. The horses drew up and the two riders climbed off. Just as Macbeth had expected, Banquo planned to walk the last mile to the palace.

Bell and Black unsheathed their knives. Banquo and Fleance walked close by the villains' hideaway, chatting amiably.

'Looks like rain,' said Banquo.

'I'll give you rain!' cried Bell, leaping out and stabbing him in the back. Blows rained down from all sides on the stricken battle hero. In their frenzy, however, the two murderers had taken their eyes off the second prize. Fleance took his chance to escape.

Bell and Black chased into the shadows, but their prey was gone.

It was a great pity that the chief guest was absent, but the banquet went ahead as planned. At the centre of it all sat the chairs of the king and queen. Everyone else took their places in order of rank. Musicians played, conversation bubbled, and Lady Macbeth revelled in the attention.

Macbeth viewed the assembled guests and felt anxious. Banquo was not the only man missing. Macduff should have been there as well. Macbeth had already heard rumours that Macduff was speaking badly of him – his absence from the feast was suspicious, to say the least.

But there were more urgent matters for the king to attend to. Bell was at the door.

'I have a small matter to attend to,' he told his guests.

'Enjoy yourselves – we'll drink together shortly.'

Macbeth took Bell into the corridor. 'There's blood on your face,' he whispered.

Bell wiped it. 'It's Banquo's,' he replied.

'He's dead?'

'His throat is cut.'

Macbeth shook Bell by the hand. 'You're the best cut-throat in the land,' he said. 'And Fleance?'

'Most royal sir,' replied Bell, 'he got away.'

Macbeth winced. 'Damn and blast!' he cried. 'Then I still cannot sleep easy!' He turned to Bell in sudden doubt. 'You're sure Banquo's dead?' he asked.

'Believe me, he could not be more dead,' replied Bell. 'Face down in the ditch, with twenty gashes to his head.'

'Very well,' said Macbeth, nodding. 'Get away now. We'll talk later.'

Lady Macbeth appeared, looking displeased. 'Macbeth!' she scolded. 'You're not paying attention to your guests!'

'Yes, all right!' snapped Macbeth. 'I've only been gone a few moments.' Then he re-entered the room with a charming smile.

'Honoured guests,' he proclaimed, 'good appetite to you all! What a dreadful shame our country's great hero, Banquo, cannot be with us. Surely he could not have deliberately let us down? Perhaps he has had difficulties.'

'Do take a seat, please, your highness,' said Lennox.

Macbeth scanned the room. Strange, but he could not see any empty chairs.

'The table's full,' he remarked.

'Here's a place reserved,' said Ross, Lady Macduff's cousin.

'Where?' asked Macbeth.

'Here, my lord!' replied Ross.

A cluster of noble hands indicated a vacant chair. Macbeth leapt back in horror. 'Which of you have done this?' he cried.

Only I shared Macbeth's vision. Only I saw, upon the chair, the dreadful spectre of Banquo, eyes dead, cut throat gaping. Saw him shake his matted locks at Macbeth as if to say 'guilty'.

'You can't say I did it!' yelled Macbeth, at the vision.

An embarrassed silence filled the hall.

'Gentlemen, rise,' said Lennox. 'His highness is not well.'

'No, no, no!' cried Lady Macbeth. 'Stay in your seats! It'll be over in a moment. My lord has had these fits since he was a child. Making a fuss about it will only make it worse.'

The guests seemed none too sure. Smiling calmly, Lady Macbeth swanned between them, ensuring their glasses were full. Eventually they were all eating again. Lady Macbeth seized her husband's arm and led him aside.

'Pull yourself together!' she hissed.

'With that in front of me?' gasped Macbeth.

'Oh, nonsense!' scolded Lady Macbeth. 'You're seeing things again. Just like that stupid dagger you blabbed on about. For heaven's sake, it's only a chair!'

'Are you blind?' said Macbeth. 'The graves are spewing back the dead!' He faced the vision again. 'Come on, you spectre!' he cried. 'You can nod, so let's hear you speak!'

Banquo rose, and melted from the scene.

'So where is this so-called spectre?' hissed Lady Macbeth.

'It was there, I tell you!' protested Macbeth.

'It's gone now, has it?' scoffed his wife.

'There was a time,' mused Macbeth, 'that when you dashed a man's brains out, that was the end of him.'

'Enough of this,' replied Lady Macbeth. 'The noble lords are waiting.'

Macbeth took a deep breath, and steadied himself. 'I'll be all right now,' he said, then turned to address the room. 'My sincere apologies,' he proclaimed. 'I have this little ailment that troubles me occasionally. Those who know me well think nothing of it. Come, let's drink to everyone's health, then I'll take my seat.'

The guests relaxed again. A few laughed. Macbeth raised his goblet.

'I drink to the happiness of all,' said Macbeth, 'and also our dear friend Banquo, whom we miss so greatly.'

'Our pledge to the king!' proclaimed the guests, raising their own goblets.

At this, Macbeth flung his wine across the table, splattering the guests, the cloth, and half a dozen dinners. 'Go, get out of my sight!' he screamed.

Banquo was back, and gorier than before.

'Go! Let the earth hide thee!' yelled Macbeth. 'Your blood is cold. Your bones have no marrow. And those eyes – those glaring eyes – there is no mind behind them!'

The guests lowered their goblets. Lady Macbeth assured them it was just another little turn, but this time there was no stopping Macbeth.

'Come back as a bear!' he cried. 'A tiger. A rhinoceros. Anything but this dreadful vision!'

Macbeth's face, the face of the great battle hero, had become the face of a frightened child. Then, just as suddenly as he had appeared, Banquo was gone again.

'Well,' said Lady Macbeth, bitterly, 'you really have ruined this party now.'

'Can you blame me?' Macbeth asked. 'With a sight like that?'

'What sight, exactly?' asked Ross, gently.

'Enough,' said Lady Macbeth. She addressed the room. 'Thank you everybody,' she said. 'You may leave now.'

Rather bewildered, and still hungry, the guests rose.

'I trust his majesty feels better soon,' said Ross.

'Don't bother with the courtesies,' snapped Lady Macbeth. 'Just go.'

The hall slowly emptied, leaving Macbeth and his wife amid the ruins of their great banquet.

'The murdered want my blood,' murmured Macbeth. 'As the saying goes, "Blood will have blood."'

'Be calm now, dearest,' said Lady Macbeth.

'I trust nobody,' continued Macbeth. 'Why wasn't

Macduff here tonight?'

'Have you contacted him?' asked his wife.

'I'll send men tomorrow,' replied Macbeth. 'And I'll visit the Weird Sisters at first light. I need to know what else I have to do. I've waded so far into this river of blood, it's easier to go further than turn back.'

'You need to sleep,' advised Lady Macbeth.

'I'm just not used to this bloody business,' said Macbeth. 'But, believe me, I will get better at it. By the time we've finished, killing men will be like swatting flies.'

CHAPTER 9

More Plots, More Prophecies

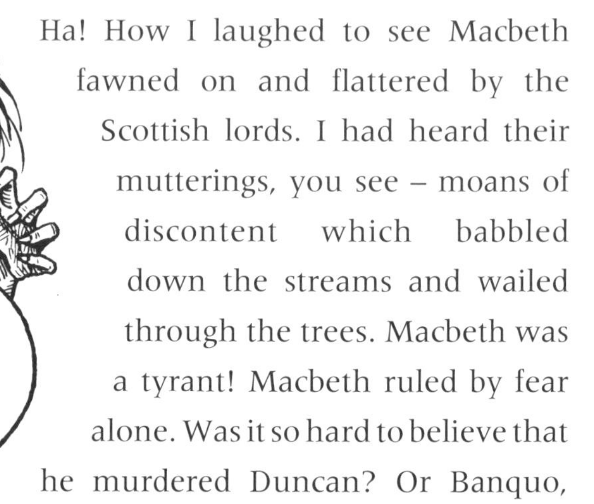

Ha! How I laughed to see Macbeth fawned on and flattered by the Scottish lords. I had heard their mutterings, you see – moans of discontent which babbled down the streams and wailed through the trees. Macbeth was a tyrant! Macbeth ruled by fear alone. Was it so hard to believe that he murdered Duncan? Or Banquo, his closest ally? A man, perhaps, who knew too much?

So, Macduff was missing from the feast. I scanned the sisters' glass hungrily for signs of his presence. There he was, with Macbeth's messengers, refusing to see the king. There he was again, on his horse, riding like a man possessed. There he was a third time, with Prince Malcolm, at the court of King Edward of England.

Macbeth was right to fear Macduff. Macduff was plotting rebellion. If he could get the English lords on Prince Malcolm's side, they would have a force to be reckoned with.

Now, however, it was time for me to sink back into the shadows. The Weird Sisters were back, with a fire, a cauldron, and a recipe from hell.

'Round about the cauldron go,' sang Cat. 'In the poisoned entrails throw!'

A stinking armful of goat's innards were flung into the pot.

'Double, double, toil and trouble,' all three sang together. 'Fire burn, and cauldron bubble.'

Next it was Hedge-pig's turn. 'Fillet of a fenny-snake,' she sang, 'in the cauldron boil and bake. Eye of newt and toe of frog, wool of bat and tongue of dog!'

The foul ingredients dropped – plop, plop, plop – into the pot.

'Double, double, toil and trouble,' came the chorus. 'Fire burn and cauldron bubble.'

Harpy came third: eyes rolling, feet frenzied. 'Cool it with a baboon's blood,' she sang, 'then the charm is firm and good.'

Harpy burst a pig's bladder against the pot, and blood gushed out like a red and putrid river. The Weird Sisters clapped and pranced and laughed like drains.

Suddenly Hedge-pig called for hush. 'By the pricking of my thumbs,' she hissed, 'something wicked this way comes.'

All was still, but for the slow bubble of the pot. A man's footsteps approached. Out of the secret mist of morning appeared Macbeth. He winced at the stench from the cauldron, and half turned his eyes from the mad-eyed bearded women.

'How now, you secret, foul and midnight hags!' he pronounced. 'What is it that you do?'

'Nothing you could name,' replied the three together.

'I have more questions for you,' said Macbeth.

'Ask away,' croaked Cat.

'You will have your answers,' added Hedge-pig.

'Would you rather they came from our mouths' asked Harpy, 'or in visions from the other side?'

'Show me the visions,' replied Macbeth.

This answer pleased the Weird Sisters. 'Come, flames,' they cried. 'Take this, the grease from a murderer's brow, as he sweated his last seconds on the scaffold.'

At this, a pungent oil was flung into the fire. There was a flash, a cloud of smoke, and a gasp from Macbeth. Above the cauldron hung a severed head in warrior's helmet – the head of Macbeth.

'Tell me, thou unknown power?' began Macbeth.

'Hush!' cried Harpy. 'He knows thy thought! Hear his

speech, but say nought.'

The mouth of the head opened. 'Macbeth!' it called, in harsh and urgent tones. 'Beware Macduff, the Thane of Fife.'

'Macduff!' cried Macbeth. 'I knew as much. One more question?'

'He will not be commanded!' cried Harpy, and sure enough, the vision faded.

'Here's another, more telling than the first,' croaked Hedge-pig.

There was a clap of thunder, and the gruesome spectre of a bloody child appeared above the cauldron. 'Macbeth! Macbeth!' it cried, in a shrill, unearthly wail.

'For pity's sake, I hear you well enough!' spluttered Macbeth.

'Be bloody and bold!' cried the vision. 'Laugh in the faces of your rivals, for no man born from a woman shall harm you.'

The bloody child vanished, leaving Macbeth with a grim smile. 'Ha!' he muttered to himself. 'No need to fear Macduff, then.'

The thunder rolled again. A third vision rose from the sisters' brew. It was a young man, with a tree in his hand, and a royal crown upon his head.

'Who are you, that dare to wear my crown?' demanded Macbeth.

'Listen, but speak not!' barked Harpy.

The crowned youth spoke. 'Macbeth shall never be defeated,' he stated, 'til Birnam Wood shall come to Dunsinane.'

Macbeth's smile returned. 'Birnam Wood come to Dunsinane?' he laughed. 'What, and walk twelve miles? That would be a sight, trees picking up their roots and walking!' He grew serious. 'Now tell me,' he demanded. 'Shall Banquo's heirs ever reign?'

'No questions!' screamed the sisters.

'Damn you, I demand to know!' cried Macbeth.

Suddenly there was a chorus of trumpets. The cauldron sank into the earth, pale smoke filled the air, and the Weird Sisters stretched out their arms and shrieked. 'Show his eyes, and pain his heart –

Come like shadows, like shadows depart!'

Out of the smoke stepped one king, then another, then another. Every single one had the look of Banquo about them. The line went on, and on, and on, ignoring the shouts and curses from Macbeth, 'til at last there stood Banquo, a grin of triumph across his bloody face.

And then they were gone.

'Macbeth!' cackled Cat. 'Why look so amazed?'

'Come on, sisters!' cried Hedge-pig. 'Let's cheer his spirits.'

The sisters began a wild and mocking dance, stroking their bony fingers through Macbeth's hair. Macbeth shook them off angrily and stormed from the scene, only to walk straight into Lennox.

'Lennox!' he snapped. 'What are you doing here? Did you see anything?'

'Nothing, my lord,' replied Lennox.

Macbeth wheeled around. The sisters were gone, and

their cauldron with them.

'We have just had word,' continued Lennox, 'that Macduff has fled to England.'

It was the last thing Macbeth wanted to hear. Grim-faced, he dismissed Lennox and addressed himself to the empty heath. 'I should have acted sooner,' he hissed. 'From now on I will waste no time thinking. And the first thing I will do is to kill every living being related to the traitorous Macduff.'

CHAPTER 10

Blood of the Innocent

Lady Macduff was beside herself. How could her husband just disappear, leaving her to cope with the castle, the servants, and the children?

Lord Ross, her cousin, did his best to console her. 'You must be patient,' he said.

'Patient?' she sighed. 'He wasn't very patient, was he?'

'He wouldn't have left without good reason,' pleaded Ross.

'How can you have a good reason to leave your wife and babies?' asked Lady Macduff.

Ross looked for the right words. This was a difficult situation. 'These are dangerous times,' he said. 'I can say no more than that.'

So Ross departed, leaving Lady Macduff no happier. James, her young son, ran to her. 'Where is daddy?' he asked.

'Daddy is dead,' replied Lady Macduff, hugging him close.

'No, he isn't dead!' protested the little lad.

'He is, I tell you,' said Lady Macduff.

James clung to his mother's skirts and buried his face. Lady Macduff stroked his fine hair. 'How will we survive, little one?' she asked.

'I will kill birds,' replied James. 'I will kill mice. And I will kill deer, and bring them home for supper.'

Lady Macduff smiled wryly at her young son's innocent hopes.

'Mummy . . .' asked James, suddenly serious. 'Was Daddy a traitor?'

'Aye,' said Lady Macduff. 'He was.'

'What is a traitor?' asked James.

'Someone who swears to love and honour,' replied his mother, bitterly, 'and lies.'

'So, if you swear and lie,' said James, 'they will hang you.'

'That's right.'

'And who will do it?'

'The honest men.'

'That's stupid!' protested James. 'Because there's more liars than honest men, so they could gang up on the honest men and hang them instead.'

Lady Macduff laughed. Her son had his own special logic; you couldn't argue with it. 'How you prattle, you monkey,' she laughed.

Without warning a strange man burst into the room, red-faced and panting. 'Bless you, fair dame!' he spluttered. 'You don't know me, but please take my advice – get out of here while you can!'

The man made his apologies and left, as quickly as he came. Lady Macduff was shocked and confused. 'Run away?' she said. 'What? I've done nothing wrong!'

Lady Macduff's hesitation was fatal. Next second, the room was full of men, grim-faced and armed to the teeth. 'Where's your husband?' barked the first.

Lady Macduff kept her nerve and stood her ground. 'Nowhere so foul that you might find him,' she replied.

'He is a traitor,' snarled the man.

Suddenly James leapt towards him, little fists flying. 'You're lying, you pig-faced goon!' he cried.

'What, you traitor's runt?' snapped the man. He drew his knife, and with one horrifying blow, ran the young lad through.

'He's killed me, Mummy!' cried James. 'Run!'

But there was no escape for Lady Macduff, or her

servants, or any of her children. The butchers did not finish their work 'til the bodies floated like driftwood in the castle moat.

CHAPTER 11

The Spark of Revolt

Back in England, Prince Malcolm was tortured by uncertainty. He had been offered the support of powerful earls such as Seyward, who alone commanded thousands of men. But Malcolm was just a teenager, with spots on his chin and self-doubt in every vein. The responsibility of being king terrified him.

'I'll be worse than Macbeth,' he complained to Macduff.

'No one could be worse than Macbeth,' replied Macduff, patiently.

'So much power,' said Malcolm. 'It will turn my head. Everything I want, I'll just take. Castles . . . jewels . . . '

'Believe me,' replied Macduff, 'when you see how much you own as king, you won't need more.'

Malcolm shifted uncomfortably. 'I'm just the wrong person to be a king,' he moaned. 'I'm not brave, I'm not patient, I'm not wise . . . '

Macduff had heard enough. 'Your father was a great man!' he cried. 'Your mother was a saint. How can their child not be fit to govern? If you're not willing to take the crown, Scotland is finished. And I am finished with Scotland.'

Macduff's words shook Malcolm. The look of self-pity left him. At this moment, Ross entered.

'Cousin!' cried Macduff.

The two men embraced.

'You bring news of Scotland?' asked Macduff.

'Still suffering,' replied Ross, sternly.

'How is my wife?' asked Macduff.

Ross looked into Macduff's eager eyes, and hesitated. 'Well,' he said.

'And the children?' asked Macduff.

'Well also,' replied Ross.

'Macbeth has not disturbed their peace, then,' said Macduff.

'They are well at peace,' replied Ross.

Macduff looked curiously at Ross's blushing face. 'What other news?' he asked.

'Men are ready to fight,' replied Ross. 'Women too.'

'Excellent,' said Macduff. 'You can tell them we are on our way. Seyward's with us, and ten thousand men.'

Ross nodded, but seemed strangely unmoved by the good news.

Something was troubling him.

'Come on, Ross,' said Macduff. 'I can see you have more to say.'

Ross breathed deeply. 'Please,' he said, 'don't blame me for bringing you this news.'

'It's bad, then,' said Macduff.

'For you, yes,' replied Ross.

'Tell me,' ordered Macduff.

'Your castle was raided,' said Ross. 'Your family have been slaughtered.'

'Merciful heavens!' cried Malcolm.

'My wife? My children too?' asked Macduff, stunned.

'Wife, children, servants . . . everyone they could find,' replied Ross.

'My pretty children!' cried Macduff. 'All I hold dear – gone!'

Malcolm rose. All his earlier doubts were forgotten. 'We must turn our grief into anger,' he proclaimed.

'Aye!' cried Macduff. 'That hell-kite will suffer for this!'

Malcolm's doubts had dissolved. 'We'll go to King Edward now,' he said. 'The army will march by the morning.'

CHAPTER 12

The Sleepwalker and the Tyrant

By now Macbeth had his spies everywhere, and it did not take long for news of the rebellion to reach him. The old Macbeth would have dithered, but the new one acted with single-minded purpose. Preparations for the defence of Dunsinane began immediately.

Lady Macbeth, meanwhile, had become a disturbing figure. She had worn two faces so long, she had grown the rigid smile of a corpse. Lady Macbeth had crushed her human nature so utterly, her body never rested. Soon, she would lose her senses completely. Doctors and attendants watched anxiously as she prowled through the night, fast asleep, eyes open.

'Must wash,' she muttered. 'Must wash.'

It was the same every night. She would rub her hands together fiercely, sometimes for twenty minutes or more.

'There's still a spot,' complained Lady Macbeth. She rubbed harder still.

'Out, damned spot!' she cried.

Now the rambling was beginning. Lady Macbeth would chatter in the most frightening way – fast and intense, like a flow of blood.

'Who would have thought the old man had such blood in him?' she railed. 'The Thane of Fife, he had a wife – where is she now, eh? Where is she now? Wash your hands, girl! Can you never get them clean? Come on now, get to bed. There's knocking at the gate. What's done is done.'

The doctors heard it all. Some said there were great truths in the ramblings of mad people. If so, it was better to keep quiet about what they had learnt. In any case, Macbeth did not want to know about it. He had banned bad news about his wife, just as he had banned bad news about the rebellion. So what if a few Scottish lords had turned traitor? thought Macbeth. So what if Malcolm was on his way? The Weird Sisters' visions assured him all would be well.

''Til Birnam Wood comes to Dunsinane,' he recalled, 'I am safe from harm. As for that pipsqueak Malcolm – was he not born from a woman? Then how can he kill me?'

Macbeth's scout was not so confident. 'Sir,' he stammered. 'There are ten thousand . . . ten thousand . . . '

'For heaven's sake!' railed Macbeth. 'Take that pathetic look off your face. You look like a white-faced goose.'

'Ten thousand soldiers, sir,' stuttered the scout.

'What was that?' snapped Macbeth. 'Ten thousand geese?'

'No, sir,' replied the terrified scout. 'The English force, so please you. They're massing at Birnam Wood.'

'Is that all?' scoffed Macbeth.

'The rebel Scots ride to meet them,' added the scout.

'Get your pale face out of here,' barked Macbeth. 'Slap it 'til the colour comes back!'

The scout backed out hurriedly. Macbeth called for Seyton, the soldier who attended on him.

'Is this true, about the English force?' rasped Macbeth.

'Yes, sir,' replied Seyton. 'We have reliable reports on it.'

Macbeth gritted his teeth. 'I'll fight them with every ounce of strength in my body!' he cried. 'Give me my armour.'

'But, sir,' protested Seyton, 'you don't need it yet.'

'I want it on!' barked Macbeth. 'And send out more scouts. Hang any Scotsman who talks of fear. Where's that damned doctor?'

A doctor hurried into the chamber.

'Is my wife any better?' demanded Macbeth.

'Not quite so sick, sir,' replied the doctor, scared to tell Macbeth the full story. 'But she is still having these turns . . . '

'You are a doctor,' said Macbeth. 'Why can't you give us an antidote for these troubles?'

'In some cases,' replied the doctor, 'the patient can only cure themselves.'

'Then throw your medicines to the dogs,' rasped Macbeth. 'Unless, of course, you can find a cure for this rebellion. Senna pods, perhaps, or syrup of figs. Anything that will purge this country of the English. You do know the English are coming?'

'I guessed as much, sir,' replied the doctor.

I smiled to see the doctor's fearful face. Like most of the court, he had only come to Dunsinane to make his fortune. Now he wished he was somewhere else – anywhere else.

CHAPTER 13

Unlucky for Some

The rebels were ready. Before the leafy glades of Birnam Wood stood a mighty army. Macbeth's attempts to stem the revolt had failed – deserters flocked in their droves to Malcolm's side. Now Macbeth's only hope was to hold on to Dunsinane.

Malcolm was growing up quickly. In place of the tortured teenager was a responsible man. He addressed the waiting army. 'We must disguise our approach,' he told them. 'Each man must cut down a leafy branch and hold it before him.'

Ten thousand soldiers obeyed his command; before the startled eyes of nature, Birnam Wood began to move. It was just as the sisters had foretold.

Back at Dunsinane, the fortifications were almost complete. Macbeth marched around the walls, ordering banners to be hung, oil to be boiled, rocks to be stacked. Before him marched a squadron of drummers in colours of war. It all looked very convincing, to those with dull eyes. But I could see into the souls of Macbeth's soldiers, and knew they had no stomach for a fight.

Macbeth, however, was like a blinkered horse; in his eyes, Dunsinane was secure.

'Let them lay siege,' he laughed. 'They'll starve before they enter these gates.'

Macbeth's band of followers laughed as well.

'Of course,' continued Macbeth, 'I would rather we took them on hand-to-hand, if they weren't stuffed full of our own men, forced to fight with that puny prince.'

There was a chorus of agreement; but then, from inside, a terrible scream, followed by an awful sound of wailing.

'What's that vile noise?' asked Macbeth.

'My good lord,' replied Seyton, 'it sounds like crying women.'

Seyton hurried inside. Macbeth stayed rooted to the spot, a curious expression on his face. He had forgotten what it was like to feel fear, or any other emotion. Now a human cry seemed strange and alien, from a land where Macbeth no longer lived.

'Well?' he asked, as Seyton returned. 'What's up?'

'The queen, my lord?' blurted Seyton.

'Yes?'

'She is dead, my lord.'

Macbeth gave a tired sigh. 'It's the wrong time to die,' he muttered. 'The wrong time altogether. Still, what does it matter? What does anything matter? Life's a joke. We puff and pant and fret and fight, and then . . . what? Where does it lead us all? To dust.'

As Macbeth spoke, so the grey blanket of sky seemed to lower, as if to smother Dunsinane. A messenger arrived, riding hectically into the castle grounds. He leapt from his horse and raced to Macbeth. Panic was written all over his face.

'My lord,' he spluttered. 'I hardly know how to say this?'

'You've got a tongue, haven't you?' snapped Macbeth.

'Sir,' the messenger went on, 'as I was standing watch, I looked up at Birnam Wood . . . and it began to move.'

'Liar and slave!' cried Macbeth, raising his arm.

The messenger cowered. 'I swear to God!' he cried. 'It's coming this way!'

'If you are lying,' warned Macbeth, 'you will hang from the nearest tree until you rot. And if not . . . God help us all.'

CHAPTER 14

The Final Reckoning

So, we had come full circle. Another foul day, another battle at hand. The stench of death would not be long coming.

Malcolm's army was organized well. They kept up their disguises 'til the castle was in their sights. Then, as one, they threw down their branches. Drums rolled and trumpets blared. The siege began.

At first it seemed the defence was sound. A rain of arrows pegged back the attackers, and boiling oil sent grown men screaming back. But sheer weight of numbers saw Malcolm gain the upper hand. The siege-hammers smashed over and over into the gates, 'til the hinges creaked and the timbers splintered. At last they gave way. Attackers poured in, hell-bent on revenge against the tyrant Macbeth. Some of the defenders fought back desperately – many fled.

Macbeth fought as he always fought – savagely. He was like a bear tied to a stake, teeth bared, sword slashing out in every direction. Again and again he reminded himself of the second prophecy – that no man born from a woman could harm him.

Soon the prophecy was put to the test. Young Seyward sprang into view – Malcolm's teenage uncle. Young Seyward was a fantastic fighter for his age. He feared no one.

'What is your name?' he ordered.

Macbeth looked down on the young man with scorn. 'You'd be terrified to hear it,' he mocked.

'Not if it were the hottest name in hell,' replied young Seyward.

'My name,' pronounced the king, 'is Macbeth.'

Young Seyward spat on the ground. 'There is no word more vile to me,' he said.

'Or more frightening,' scoffed Macbeth.

Young Seyward raised his sword. 'We'll soon see about that,' he replied.

The two men rushed together. Young Seyward's sword smashed into Macbeth's armoured breast. But Macbeth had taken harder blows than that. In an instant he was back at young Seyward. The youth was certainly brave, but Macbeth was a hundred times more canny. In less than a minute it was all over, and young Seyward was dead.

'Ha!' panted Macbeth. 'Another man born of woman. You're all wasting your time. Your swords are useless against me.'

Macbeth's army was not so lucky. Those who did not

flee lay dead at their posts, while a final few fought a last desperate battle. If Macbeth had had any sense, he would have fallen on his sword. Instead he threw himself back into the fray like a man possessed.

Meanwhile, another warrior stalked the castle. Like Macbeth, his eyes were fixed before him, and his mind was set on one sole purpose. His name was Macduff.

◆◆◆

Malcolm surveyed the scene inside the castle gates. The savagery of battle appalled him. Old Seyward, meanwhile, had seen it all before.

'To rid ourselves of Macbeth,' he said, 'this is a price worth paying.'

Ross rushed to greet them. 'The day is as good as ours,' he proclaimed.

'Is Macbeth alive?' asked Malcolm.

'By some miracle,' replied Ross.

'Then the battle is not yet won,' said Malcolm.

'What of my son?' asked old Seyward, anxiously.

'Your son,' replied Ross, 'has paid a soldier's debt.'

Old Seyward was a hard man. He showed no emotion. There was only one thing that concerned him. 'Where were his wounds?' he asked.

'On the front,' replied Ross.

'In that case,' said old Seyward, 'he could not have had a better death.'

Malcolm winced.

Macbeth pulled his blooded sword from another English wretch, then spun to face the next enemy. Before him, like fate itself, stood Macduff.

'Greetings, hell-hound,' rasped Macduff.

Macbeth lowered his sword. 'Get away,' he said. 'I've

had too much of your blood already.'

'You filthy savage!' cried Macduff. He ran at Macbeth in a vengeful fury. Macbeth fought him back.

'You're wasting your time!' cried Macbeth. 'I lead a charmed life. No man born from a woman can kill me.'

Macduff's face broke into a savage grin. 'Is that so?' he scoffed. 'Well, Macbeth, your charmed life is about to end. I, Macduff, was never naturally born. Surgeons cut me from my mother's womb.'

At these words the confidence drained from Macbeth. 'I don't want to fight you, Macduff,' he said.

'Then yield,' replied Macduff.

'What, and be dragged before a howling crowd?' said Macbeth. 'To kiss Malcolm's feet?'

'To be stuck on a pole,' hissed Macduff, 'with "See the tyrant" written underneath.'

'I will fight to the end,' declared Macbeth. 'Do your worst, Macduff!'

The warriors rushed together, like snarling terriers, in a last-ditch struggle. Macbeth's strength was superhuman, but no one had fought back like Macduff. The blood of his innocent children fuelled his every blow. They fought across the courtyard into the view of Malcolm and old Seyward. Macduff fell back inside the castle. Macbeth pursued him.

There was a cry, unearthly as a devil's shriek. The door

opened. Out walked Macduff, bearing the severed head of the tyrant king.

'Hail, King Malcolm!' he cried.

There was a mighty cheer, and the victorious army took up Macduff's cry.

So ended the story of Macbeth, and, for now, my interest in the sisters' glass. Malcolm, I was sure, would reward his friends as all kings do, and reign happily for a long time. After that, as the sisters foretold, Fleance would be king, then his son, then his son, and so on. But the memory of Macbeth and his fiendish wife would live as long.

GLOSSARY

Awe	wonder or amazement
Bedchamber	an old word for bedroom
Coronation	a ceremony in which a man or a woman is crowned king or queen
Hail	a formal way of saying hello
Heath	a wild, flat area without trees, sometimes covered in heather
Kinsman	a person related to you by blood, or by community
Loch	a Scottish word for a lake
Prophecy	a prediction of what will happen in the future
Shroud	a thin veil used to cover a dead body
Thane	a Scottish noble, chief of a clan

CHARACTERS IN THE STORY

Macbeth
(Cousin to King Duncan, Thane of Glamis, Thane of Cawdor, king)

Lady Macbeth
(Macbeth's wife, queen)

Banquo
(Scottish lord)

Narrator

Fleance
(Banquo's son)

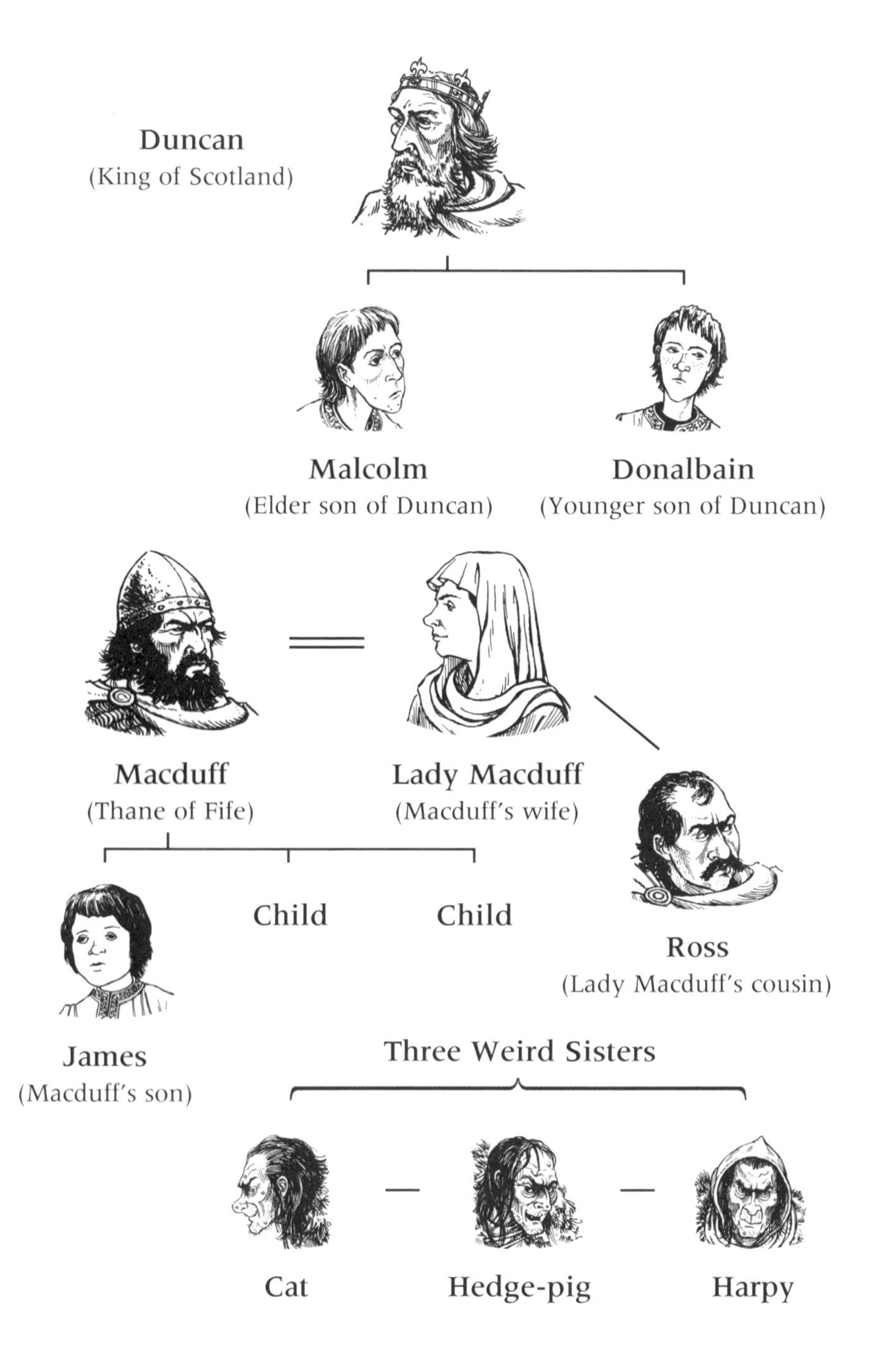
Duncan
(King of Scotland)
Malcolm
(Elder son of Duncan)
Donalbain
(Younger son of Duncan)
Macduff
(Thane of Fife)
Lady Macduff
(Macduff's wife)
Ross
(Lady Macduff's cousin)
James
(Macduff's son)
Child
Child
Three Weird Sisters
Cat
Hedge-pig
Harpy